IN CELEBRATION OF

GUESTS

NAME	NOTE

GUESTS

NAME	NOTE

GUESTS

NAME	NOTE

GUESTS

NAME	NOTE

GUESTS

NAME	NOTE

GUESTS

NAME

NOTE

GUESTS

NAME	NOTE

GUESTS

NAME	NOTE

GUESTS

NAME

NOTE

GUESTS

NAME	NOTE

GUESTS

NAME	NOTE

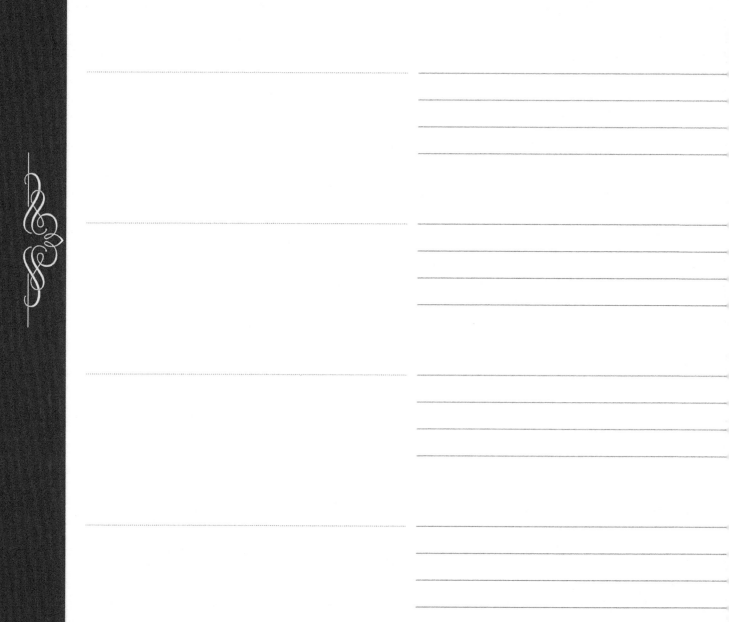

GUESTS

NAME	NOTE

GUESTS

NAME	NOTE

GUESTS

NAME	NOTE

GUESTS

NAME	NOTE

GUESTS

NAME

NOTE

GUESTS

NAME	NOTE

GUESTS

NAME

NOTE

GUESTS

NAME	NOTE

GUESTS

NAME	NOTE

GUESTS

NAME

NOTE

GUESTS

NAME

NOTE

GUESTS

NAME	NOTE

GUESTS

NAME

NOTE

GUESTS

NAME	NOTE

GUESTS

NAME

NOTE

GUESTS

NAME

NOTE

GUESTS

NAME	NOTE

GUESTS

NAME

NOTE

GUESTS

NAME

NOTE

GUESTS

NAME	NOTE

GUESTS

NAME	NOTE

GUESTS

NAME	NOTE

GUESTS

NAME

NOTE

GUESTS

NAME	NOTE

GUESTS

NAME	NOTE

GUESTS

NAME	NOTE

GUESTS

NAME	NOTE

GUESTS

NAME	NOTE

GUESTS

NAME	NOTE

GUESTS

NAME	NOTE

GUESTS

NAME

NOTE

GUESTS

NAME	NOTE

GUESTS

NAME

NOTE

GUESTS

NAME	NOTE

GUESTS

NAME	NOTE

GUESTS

NAME	NOTE

GUESTS

NAME

NOTE

GUESTS

NAME	NOTE

GUESTS

NAME

NOTE

GUESTS

NAME	NOTE

GUESTS

NAME

NOTE

GUESTS

NAME	NOTE

GUESTS

NAME

NOTE

GUESTS

NAME	NOTE

GUESTS

NAME   NOTE

GUESTS

NAME	NOTE

GUESTS

NAME

NOTE

GUESTS

NAME	NOTE

GUESTS

NAME	NOTE

GUESTS

NAME

NOTE

GUESTS

NAME

NOTE

GUESTS

NAME	NOTE

GUESTS

NAME	NOTE

GUESTS

NAME

NOTE

GUESTS

NAME

NOTE

GUESTS

NAME	NOTE

GUESTS

NAME

NOTE

GUESTS

NAME	NOTE

GUESTS

NAME

NOTE

GUESTS

NAME	NOTE

GUESTS

NAME   NOTE

GUESTS

NAME

NOTE

GUESTS

NAME

NOTE

GUESTS

NAME	NOTE

GUESTS

NAME	NOTE

GUESTS

NAME

NOTE

GUESTS

NAME

NOTE

GUESTS

NAME	NOTE

GUESTS

NAME   NOTE

GUESTS

NAME	NOTE

GUESTS

NAME

NOTE

GUESTS

NAME	NOTE

GUESTS

NAME

NOTE

GUESTS

NAME	NOTE

GUESTS

NAME	NOTE

GUESTS

NAME	NOTE

GUESTS

NAME	NOTE

GUESTS

NAME

NOTE

GUESTS

NAME

NOTE

GUESTS

NAME	NOTE

GUESTS

NAME	NOTE

GUESTS

NAME

NOTE

GUESTS

NAME

NOTE

GUESTS

NAME	NOTE

GUESTS

NAME	NOTE

GUESTS

NAME	NOTE

GUESTS

NAME

NOTE

GUESTS

NAME	NOTE

Made in the USA
Monee, IL
18 July 2022

99922912R00057